LIFE ON THE REEF

Contents

by Andy Belcher

 CAMBRIDGE UNIVERSITY PRESS

 UCL Institute of Education

WHAT ARE CORALS?

A coral reef is made up of thousands of tiny creatures called polyps living very close together. They have a hard outer skeleton like a snail's **shell**.

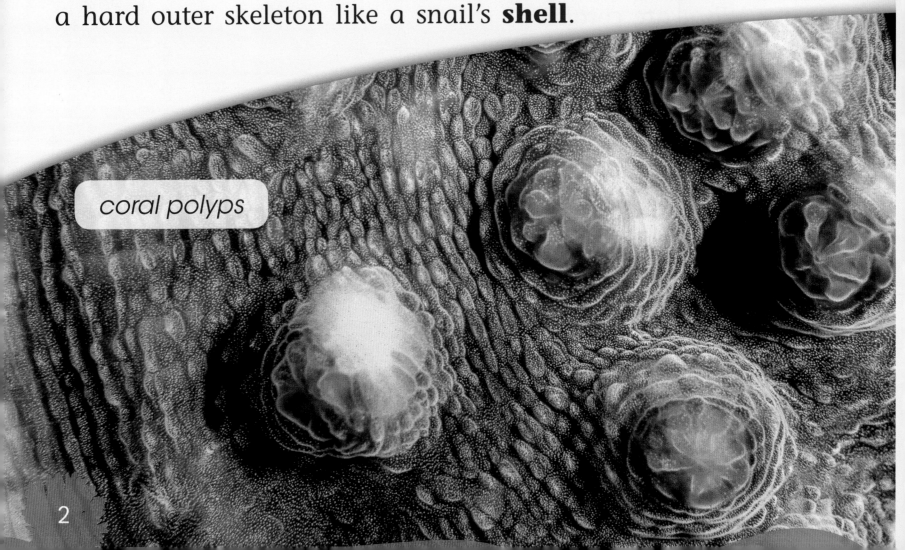

coral polyps

Corals are lots of shapes, sizes and colours.
Soft corals move with the sea **current**.
Hard corals cannot move.

hard corals

WHERE IN THE WORLD?

Coral reefs have been growing for about ten thousand years. They cover a very small part of the world's oceans.

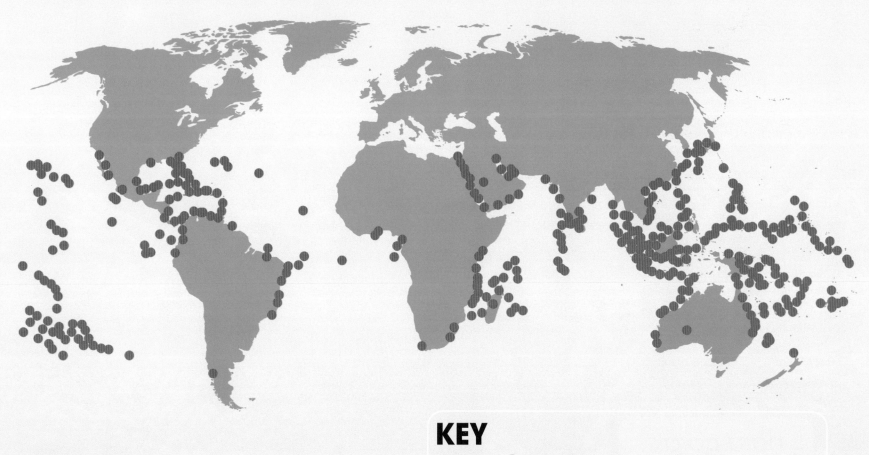

KEY
• coral reefs around the world

They grow best in sunny places with shallow water. Coral reefs can also grow on old sunken **shipwrecks**.

a reef in shallow water

a shipwreck covered in coral

TEEMING WITH LIFE

Many different creatures live on coral reefs and they need each other. Fish eat **parasites** off the reef. This keeps the reef clean.

Yellow striped snapper swim close to the reef to keep safe.

Small fish hide from larger fish so they won't get eaten.

Fish can hide in the coral.

TYPES OF FISH

The Long-nosed Hawkfish rests on the coral.
The sea current brings it tasty meals
like shrimps and prawns.

This fish is waiting for dinner.

These Barracuda swim together in schools.
They can attack fish bigger than themselves.

a school of Barracuda

UNUSUAL FISH

These tiny fish swim head down. They can dart quickly into the coral in case of danger.

Razor fish

These fish look like dead leaves. If smaller fish come too close they will get eaten.

two Leaf Fish

11

STRANGE ANIMALS

This crab covers itself with bits of coral so it is harder to see.

a Decorator Crab

This fish spreads its **fins** to fly along the bottom.

a Flying Gurnard

This crab has a soft body and lives in a shell. As it grows it needs to find a larger empty shell to live in.

a Hermit Crab

Eels open their mouths and tiny shrimps clean their teeth.

a Moray Eel

ANIMALS THAT HUNT ON THE REEF

This big fish has no teeth. It sucks in and swallows fish and octopus.

a big Grouper

Sharks are hunters. They eat some
of the larger fish on the reef.

ANIMALS THAT EAT THE REEF

Turtles eat plants and **algae**. They must come to the surface to breathe.

a turtle eating

This starfish has **poisonous spines** and eats the coral.

a Crown of Thorns Starfish

SAVING THE REEF

Coral reefs are special. We must look after them. Don't drop your anchor on the reef. It will break the coral.

broken coral

Don't throw your rubbish in the ocean. The creatures may swallow it and die. **Marine** reserves will save our coral reefs. We can look at the marine life but nothing can be taken or touched.

A big storm has washed this rubbish up on the beach.

GLOSSARY

algae - plants with no stem or leaves that grow in or near water

current - natural flow of water in one direction

fins - thin, triangular parts on a fish that help it to swim

marine - related to the sea

parasite - creature that lives off another creature

poisonous - containing poison

shell - hard outer covering of some creatures

shipwrecks - ships that have been sunk

spines - long, sharp point like needles growing out of an animal

INDEX

LIFE ON THE REEF  Andy Belcher

Teaching notes written by Sue Bodman and Glen Franklin

Using this book

Developing reading comprehension

This non-fiction report provides the opportunity to learn about life on a coral reef. Enjoying the stunning photography, children can find out about the many creatures that make the reef their home.

Grammar and sentence structure

- Sentence structures are more formal than those used in fiction texts at this band, using language common in the report genre.

- Longer complex sentences often provide more than one piece of information.

Word meaning and spelling

- The text uses many pronouns ('this', 'these', 'they'). The precise interpretation of the subject of these pronouns may be challenging for some learners, particularly those learning English.

- Technical vocabulary associated with the topic is used. Although well supported by illustration, understanding of this vocabulary may need supporting when introducing this text.

Curriculum links

Art – the stunning photography in this book provides the opportunity to follow up the reading with observational drawings. These could then be labelled using the information in the book.

Geography – page 4 tells us where in the world reefs can be found. Choose one of those areas and find out more about it. What fish can be found there? Are there any wrecks? Find out more from the internet.

Learning outcomes

Children can:

- infer meaning from the text
- read longer phrases and more complex sentences
- attend to a greater range of punctuation
- search for and use familiar inflectional endings (ed) to read past tense words.

A guided reading lesson

Book Introduction

Give each child a book and read the title to them.

Orientation

Say: *This is a non-fiction text. It will help us find out about coral reefs and all the creatures that live there.* Draw out what the children know about coral reefs already. Use the discussion to formulate one or two questions that the children want to find out. Jot down their questions on flipchart paper.

Preparation

Pages 2 and 3: Read the text on these pages aloud to the children. Then discuss with them what they noticed; the layout, the labels, the use of photographs for example.

Browse through the pages, pointing out how additional information is given in the labels and how words in bold are to be found in the glossary.

Practise reading unfamiliar vocabulary (for example, *'polyps'*, *'current'*, *'marine'*, the names of the fish) so that the children can read independently.

Set a purpose for reading: *Think about the questions we have asked as you read. We will be talking about all the things we learned after we have read the book.*